Award Winning Low-Fat Afghani Cooking

by Asad Gharwal

Cover Design: Terry Dugan
Cover Photography: Terry Dugan
Interior Design: Claire Lewis

Asad Gharwal
Da Afghan Restaurant
929 West 80th St.
Bloomington, MN   55420
FAX 1 (612) 888-3067
1 (612) 888-5824

Table of Contents

Acknowledgements

I could not have put this cookbook together without the help of others. I would like to thank my wife, Palwasha, for writing the recipes on paper, which was a considerable effort because our recipes have been handed down from generation to generation but seldom written down.

Many thanks go to Pamela Eifert for compiling the information for the cookbook, as well as testing many of the recipes herself.

I would also like to thank all of my customers who expressed so much interest in the cookbook and inspired me to finish it.

About the Author

I was born in Kabul, the capital of Afghanistan, in 1958. I grew up in a large family where daily food preparation was done on a large scale. Everything cooked in our home was homemade, we even had our own cows for milk and making yogurt and cheese.

My mother's side of the family was especially good at cooking. In addition to feeding a family household, my mother was also responsible for preparing food for my father's business guests. We had a guest house next to our house where my father's business associates could stay when they were in the area. My mother often cooked for 20 to 30 guests each day. Afghanistan does not have many restaurants and most entertaining is done in the home.

While my father did not know very much about cooking he did teach me a lot about business. He was a very successful businessman who embedded in me a strong work ethic.

While growing up I spent a lot of time with my grandfather on my mother's side. Although it is not typical for men to cook in Afghanistan, my grandfather enjoyed it as a hobby. He had a special touch with food and everything he made was very delicious. Our family had a summer home in Jalalabad, in the southern region of Afghanistan, and I often traveled there with him on weekends. I helped him cook and learned how to make several different kinds of foods.

My life changed drastically in 1979 when the Soviet Union invaded Afghanistan. While the Soviet Union was in occupation of my country, I was drafted, which meant I was expected to fight alongside the Soviets against my own people. In

December I escaped the Soviets and found my way to America, bringing with me my newly married wife, Palwasha.

I came to Minnesota where a relative was living. I got a job working at a restaurant in a major hotel in the Twin Cities. At this time I was also learning English and going to school at the University of Minnesota. I worked at the restaurant for several years and learned how to run a restaurant.

In 1988 I decided to introduce Afghani food (our own family recipes) to the Twin Cities and opened Da Afghan Restaurant. The first month after I opened the restaurant, we were nominated as having the best ethnic restaurant in the Minneapolis and St. Paul area by the *Twin Cities Reader*. We also received this award in 1990 and 1994. Opening and running the restaurant took a lot of hard work and still does. The hard work, combined with good food, has made the restaurant a success.

I got the idea to put together this cookbook two years ago when several customers of the restaurant requested recipes. Since so many people were interested in learning how to prepare Afghani cuisine, I began giving cooking lessons at the restaurant on weekends. The lessons were very successful and students were given typed recipes of what they had prepared. We had already typed up several of the recipes and found we were already on our way to putting together a whole cookbook.

Asad Gharwal

A Note to the Health Conscious

The recipes in this cookbook complement a healthy lifestyle. Afghan cooking is low in fat, cholesterol and sugar. We use lots of fresh fruits and vegetables, lean meats, and low-fat dairy products in our cooking.

All chicken used in the recipes is skinless with excess fat removed. We recommend using meat containing the lowest amount of fat, and suggest you cut off any excess fat showing on any meat before cooking it.

We use corn oil or vegetable oil, which contains little or no cholesterol. No butter is used in any of our recipes (with the exception of baklava).

While we give a recommended amount of salt to use in the recipes, those of you wanting to reduce your sodium intake can either reduce the amount or substitute low sodium salt.

Healthy food does not have to be bland and boring to be good for you. We use a combination of herbs, spices, fresh vegetables and yogurt to make sauces that are rich and satisfying, yet low in calories.

Introduction —
History of Afghan Cooking, Climate and Traditions

History of Afghan Food

Afghani people take pride in their cooking and their family recipes that have been passed down from one generation to the next for over one thousand years. Afghani food is rich in flavors, including coriander, cardamom, cayenne pepper, curry, garlic, mint, homemade yogurt, fresh fruits and vegetables, as well as many others.

Much of the history of Afghan cooking has been influenced by other countries. Because Afghanistan was a major crossroads for invaders, including Alexander the Great and Genghis Khan, as well as traders and merchants traveling the ancient Silk Route, a variety of spices and cooking techniques were introduced to the Afghani people. Major influences were adopted from China, India, Greece and the Middle Eastern countries.

Climate and Agriculture

Afghanistan is located in southwestern Asia. Bordering countries include the former Soviet Union, Iran, Pakistan and China. Much of the country has a rugged terrain and harsh climate. The middle of the country is covered with mountains, the highest peaks reaching 7,000 feet above sea level. The western and southern portions of the country are deserts. While the summers are hot and dry, the winters are cold, with some areas receiving heavy snowfall. It is from this heavy snowfall that Afghanistan receives much of its water. Over the centuries people have learned to irrigate the water to grow a variety of crops. The main crops are wheat, corn, rice, fruits, nuts, and vegetables.

Afghan Customs and Traditions

Traditionally, women prepare the food in Afghanistan. Girls begin to learn how to cook when they are about 10 years old. By the time they are 12 or 13 they can cook most basic dishes. Girls also help their mothers take care of the home and younger children.

Most families eat on the floor in a large family room. The floors are covered with large, beautiful rugs, for which Afghanistan is famous. A large cloth called a disterkhan is laid out on the floor and is what the food is placed on for the meal. People sit cross legged on long colorful cushions and pillows. Before the meal is served the host or youngest adult brings water and soap so everyone can wash their hands. The water is poured from a large jug held over a bowl. This process is also repeated after the meal.

A typical meal would include naan bread, homemade chutney sauces and jam, a vegetable salad, a chicken dish with rice, a pasta dish, and pickled vegetables. Unlike Americans, Afghans usually serve several entrees at one meal. All food is placed on the disterkhan and is served at one time. Traditionally, Afghans shared food served on large platters and used their fingers to eat. Today, large ornate platters are still used to serve food, but individual plates and silverware are also used. Water, lemonade, and yogurt drinks are typical beverages at mealtime.

Usually a family will eat together, but if guests outside of the family are present, the men and women will eat in separate areas. It is not appropriate for men outside of the family to see the women. In these instances, a young male adult will serve the meal to the men.

When guests are present they are honored very much by their host. The very best foods, dishes and clothes are used. The guest is given the choicest pieces of meats and other foods.

About the Kitchen —
Herbs, Spices, Seasonings and Special Ingredients

Basmati Rice is a long grain rice grown in India. It is often available at supermarkets, but can also be purchased at an Indian or Asian grocery store.

Black Tea refered to in this cookbook is used in the recipe for Shir Chiy. We use a ground black tea from Calcutta, India called Brooke Bond Red Label Tea. This tea can be purchased from an Indian, Asian or Greek grocery store.

Bulgur Wheat is a cracked wheat. There are several different grades of bulgur wheat available. For the recipes in this cookbook, use size #1, which is cracked very small. You will most likely need to purchase this at an ethnic grocery store.

Cardamom Seeds are the fruit or seeds of a plant in the ginger family, native to India. There are three types of cardamom: green, white and black. White cardamom is used in the recipes in this book. It has a pleasant pungent aroma and sweet flavor. Cardamom is a popular spice throughout the Arab and Scandinavian countries. It is used to flavor sweet pastries, breads, cakes, cookies and coffee. Cardamom has a better flavor when it comes from seeds, rather than powder. Crush seeds before using. Available at most grocery stores.

Cayenne Pepper is the ground dried pod of the small, more pungent, varieties of chili peppers. Its orange to bright red color well represents its fiery character.

Chick Peas or Garbanzo Beans are legumes. They are high in fiber and low in fat.

Cilantro, also known as Chinese parsley. It is used in cooking in Mexico, India and China. Cilantro has a unique smell and flavor, and is an acquired taste. It is available at your local grocery store.

Coriander comes from the seeds of cilantro. Ground coriander seeds are often used in Afghan baking and give vegetable dishes special flavor.

Curry has an exotic aroma and spicy flavor. Curry is not a single spice but a blend, including coriander, fenugreek, turmeric, cumin, red peppers and other strong spices. It originated from the cooking of India. It is often used with sauces, eggs, cheeses, meats, fish and poultry. It is also added to marinades for lamb, beef, chicken, and fish.

Dill Weed. The dill weed leaf is milder in flavor than the seed. And its bright green color makes it a great garnish. Dill is widely used in Scandinavian and Russian cooking.

Garam Masala is a combination of five spices: black cardamom, black peppercorns, cloves, coriander and cinnamon. This spice is derived from India. Available at Indian or Asian grocery stores.

Garlic is very popular and is used in a variety of dishes across the world, both as a flavoring and for medicinal purposes. Crushed garlic cooked for a long period in a soup or simmered dish gives a rich flavor to the sauce but is not overwhelming.

Ginger Root is a beige colored root that adds a unique taste of its own. It is available at most grocery stores.

Lemon Juice. Always use fresh lemon juice when possible. Lemon juice sharpens the taste of many dishes.

Mint. The leaves from this aromatic plant make an excellent garnish and flavoring for foods. Used fresh and dried.

Mung Beans are small beans green in color. You will find these at an ethnic grocery store.

Paprika is the mildest member of the Capsicum pepper family. It was discovered by Christopher Columbus in the New World. Grown in California, its bright red color makes it a pleasing garnish.

Rose Water is made of roses distilled with water. It has a distinctive, delicate flavor often used in desserts of Middle Eastern cooking.

Salt adds its own flavor and also helps bring out the other flavors in food.

Saffron. The deep orange aromatic pungent dried stigmas of saffron have been used to color and flavor foods and formerly were used as a dyestuff and in medicines. Never use more saffron than required. Before using saffron it must be steeped in hot liquid to bring out its flavor.

Tahini is made from ground sesame seeds. It is used in many Middle Eastern foods. Available at your local specialty food store.

Yogurt is fermented milk. Yogurt is widely used in Afghani cooking. It is eaten plain, with fruit, and with several dishes. Yogurt is low in calories, economical and easy to make.

About the Kitchen —
Cooking Terms and Techniques

Bake. To prepare by dry heat. Always preheat oven 10-15 minutes before baking. Do not overcrowd by placing too many items in oven.

Barbecue. To roast or broil on a rack over hot coals.

Blend. To incorporate two or more ingredients thoroughly, either with an electric mixer or by hand.

Boil. To heat a liquid until bubbles break continuously on the surface.

Brown. Brown meat and vegetables in a frying pan with oil or oil substitute. The purpose is to sear, to seal in juices and to give a browned color. When browning several items do not overcrowd pan or you will be steaming, not browning.

Chop. To cut items with a sharp knife or chopping tool into small pieces. Hold a chopping knife at both ends and repeatedly bring blade up and down over item until chopped into small pieces.

Dice. To slice items into small cubes. First, make horizontal cuts at even intervals, not cutting all the way through. Second, make vertical slices, again not cutting all the way through. Last, slice straight down so that small cubes of item fall away.

Fry. Cooking in a frying pan with oil. It is important that the oil is hot enough so the foods do not absorb it and become greasy. Thoroughly dry items before adding to oil or the oil will splatter.

Garnish. To decorate and improve the appearance of a dish, as well as the taste.

Grind. Use a pestle and mortar to grind herbs and spices.

Marinate. To submerge food in a seasoned liquid. Marinating food will add flavor and tenderize meats.

Mix. To combine two or more ingredients.

Peel. To remove the peels from fruits and vegetables.

Pinch. A small amount of an ingredient you can hold between your thumb and forefinger.

Saute. Requires less oil and a lower heat than frying—gently cooking item.

Simmer. To boil gently. There should be only small bubbles appearing at top of liquid.

Slice. To slice an onion: Peel outer layer of skin. Cut onion in half. Lay each half on its flat side. With a sharp knife thinly slice onion so that each piece is an arc.

Steep. To pour boiling water over something and let it sit.

Appetizers

Spinach Dip

1 large bunch fresh spinach
1 medium yellow onion
2 teaspoons crushed garlic
1/4 cup corn oil
2 cups plain yogurt
1/8 teaspoon cayenne pepper
1/2 teaspoon salt
1/4 teaspoon black pepper
1/2 teaspoon freshly ground coriander seeds

1. Wash spinach and chop into small pieces.

2. In a medium sized saucepan cook spinach in about an inch of water. Cook for approximately 5 minutes or until spinach is wilted. Drain water.

3. Peel and chop onion.

4. Heat oil in a frying pan over medium-high heat and saute chopped onion and garlic.

5. Add spinach and cook for 2-3 minutes. Remove from heat and cool.

6. Mix together yogurt, spinach mixture, salt, pepper, coriander and cayenne pepper. Refrigerate overnight.

To Serve: with naan or pita bread.

Hummous
(Bean Dip)

2 15-oz. cans chick peas or garbanzo beans
(drained)
4 tablespoons tahini
2 teaspoons crushed garlic
1/2 lemon, fresh squeezed
1 teaspoon salt
3 tablespoons water
1/4 cup plain yogurt
Garnish:
1 tablespoon olive oil
paprika

1. Put all ingredients except garnish into a blender and blend until smooth.

To Serve: Spread dip on a platter, top with olive oil and a pinch of paprika. Serve with naan or pita bread.

Boulanee Spinach
(Spinach Filled Turnovers)

1 bunch green onions
1 bunch fresh spinach
1 bunch cilantro
1 tablespoon olive oil
1/2 teaspoon salt
1 teaspoon freshly ground coriander seeds
1/8 teaspoon cayenne pepper
1/4 teaspoon black pepper
1 package eggroll skins
corn oil

1. Wash green onions, spinach and cilantro. Drain well and chop very fine.

2. In a large bowl combine the greens, spices and olive oil.

3. To wrap the eggrolls, place the eggroll skin on working surface. Place a portion of the filling in the middle of the eggroll skin. Dip a finger in water and lightly wet edges of eggroll skin. Fold eggroll in half to form triangle and seal edges. (Variations can be made by cutting eggroll skins into different shapes and sizes.)

4. Heat a small amount (1 tablespoon) of corn oil in large frying pan over medium heat. Saute boulanee 4-5 minutes until lightly browned. Add more oil to pan as necessary.

To Serve: with yogurt sauce, or a tomato or cilantro chutney sauce.

Lamb Ribs

2 pounds lamb ribs
Marinade:
1/2 yellow onion, sliced
1 teaspoon crushed garlic
1 teaspoon freshly ground coriander seeds
1/4 teaspoon black pepper
1 teaspoon salt
1 tablespoon corn oil

1. Cut the lamb ribs into 4-5 inch pieces.

2. Mix together the ingredients for the marinade. Cover the ribs with the marinade and refrigerate 2 hours.

3. Cook on barbecue over medium coals for 10-15 minutes.

To Serve: with cilantro and tomato chutney sauces.

Boulanee Katchalu
(Potato Filled Turnovers)

4 large potatoes
1/2 bunch cilantro, chopped
1/2 bunch green onions, chopped
1 teaspoon salt
1/2 teaspoon black pepper
1/4 teaspoon cayenne pepper
1 teaspoon freshly ground coriander seeds
1 package eggroll skins
corn oil

1. Wash the potatoes and boil for 20 minutes or until tender.

2. Drain the water, peel potatoes and mash thoroughly.

3. Mix in all spices, green onions and cilantro.

4. To wrap the eggrolls, place the eggroll skin on working surface. Place a portion of the potato filling in the middle of the eggroll skin. Dip a finger in water and lightly wet edges of eggroll skin. Fold eggroll in half to form triangle and seal edges. Potato filling should be approximately 1/4 inch thick inside eggroll skin. (Variations can be made by cutting eggroll skins into different shapes and sizes.)

5. Heat a small amount (1 tablespoon) of corn oil in large frying pan over medium heat. Saute boulanee 4-5 minutes until lightly browned. Add more oil to pan as necessary.

To Serve: with yogurt sauce, or a tomato or cilantro chutney sauce.

Pakawra
(Deep Fried Battered Vegetables)

1 large white potato
1 eggplant
1 zucchini
1 cup corn oil
Batter:
1 1/4 cups water
1 cup flour
1 teaspoon salt
1 teaspoon black pepper
1 teaspoon freshly ground coriander seeds
1 tablespoon paprika
1 teaspoon fresh garlic
1 teaspoon baking soda
1/2 teaspoon cayenne pepper

1. Prepare batter 30 minutes ahead of time. Mix the flour and water with an electric hand mixer. Add spices and mix well. Cover and put in refrigerator for 30 minutes.

2. Peel vegetables and slice into 1/4 inch round pieces.

3. Heat oil in a large deep frying pan (oil should be approximately 1/2 inch deep).

4. Dip the vegetable slices in the batter and then fry in hot oil for 4-5 minutes until lightly browned.

To Serve: with your choice of yogurt sauce, or a tomato or cilantro chutney sauce.

Sambosa
(Beef Filled Pastries)

1 pound ground beef -90% lean
1 medium yellow onion, chopped
1 green or red bell pepper, chopped
1 teaspoon crushed garlic
1 cup water
1 teaspoon salt
1 teaspoon black pepper
1 teaspoon freshly ground coriander seeds
2 boxes puff pastry sheets

Note: This recipe makes approximately 36 sambosas. You can make them ahead of time and freeze them. Thaw before baking.

Preheat oven to 350 degrees.

1. Saute the ground beef in a medium sized frying pan over medium-high heat until browned.

2. Add the garlic, salt, black pepper, onion, bell pepper, coriander and water to meat mixture and cook over medium heat until the water is reduced.

3. Thaw puff pastry sheets for approximately 20 minutes before using. Cut the puff pastry into 2-inch squares.

4. Fill the center of each square with a heaping teaspoon of the ground beef mixture. Fold the pastry into a triangle, and gently press the edges together.

5. Bake sambosas on a large cookie sheet for 20-25 minutes at 350 degrees until lightly browned and the pastry is puffed up.

To Serve: with yogurt sauce.

Baba Ghanoush
(Eggplant Dip)

2 medium eggplants
3 tablespoons tahini
1 teaspoon crushed garlic
1/2 teaspoon salt
1/2 teaspoon black pepper
1/2 fresh squeezed lemon
2 tablespoons plain yogurt
Garnish:
1 tablespoon olive oil
paprika
parsley

Preheat oven to 375 degrees.

1. Punch small holes into eggplants, wrap in aluminum foil and bake in oven at 375 degrees for 1 hour.

2. Remove from oven and skin eggplants.

3. Mash eggplants and chill.

4. Mix together all ingredients except garnish.

To Serve: Spread on a serving plate and spoon olive oil over the top. Sprinkle with paprika and chopped parsley. Serve with naan bread.

Stuffed Zucchini

4 small/medium zucchini
Meat Mixture:
3/4 pound ground beef—90% lean
1/2 medium yellow onion, chopped
1/2 green or red bell pepper, chopped
1 teaspoon crushed garlic
3 tablespoons tomato paste
1/2 cup water
1/2 teaspoon salt
1/4 teaspoon black pepper
1 teaspoon freshly ground coriander seeds
Korma Sauce:
(See page 94)

Preheat oven to 350 degrees.

1. Saute ground beef and chopped onion in a large frying pan over medium-high heat until browned. Add remaining ingredients for meat mixture to frying pan and simmer until water reduces.

2. Wash zucchini, cut each in half lengthwise and scoop out centers. Chop centers and add to meat mixture..

3. Stuff center of each zucchini with meat mixture. Add 1/2 cup water to bottom of pan, and cover with foil.

4. Bake for approximately 35-45 minutes in a large shallow baking dish sprayed with Pam® cooking spray.

To Serve: Spread korma sauce over the top of each zucchini.

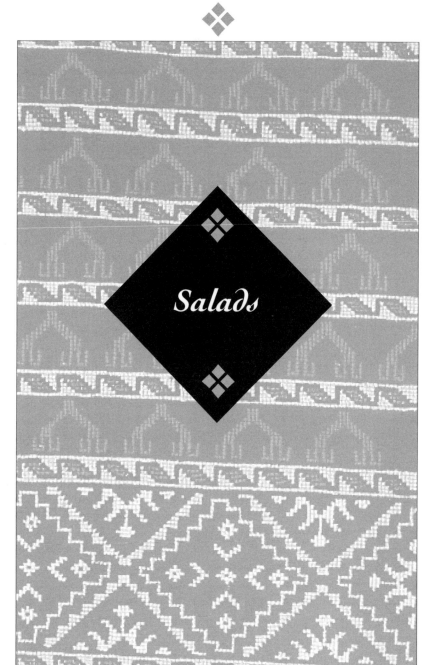

Salads

Red Onion & Tomato Salad

1 red onion, chopped
2 large tomatoes, chopped
1 teaspoon black pepper
1 teaspoon salt
2 tablespoons apple cider vinegar

1. Mix all ingredients together in a medium sized bowl.
2. Marinate for 10 minutes before serving.

Cherry Salad

1 cup fresh dark cherries, pitted
1 cup plain yogurt
1 small clove garlic, crushed
1/4 teaspoon salt
Garnish:
cilantro or parsley

1. Wash cherries, remove pits and chop lengthwise.
2. Crush the garlic and mix with cherries, yogurt and salt.

To Serve: Sprinkle with chopped parsley or cilantro.

Chicken Salad

1 pound boneless chicken breast
1/4 head Romaine lettuce, chopped
1/4 head leaf lettuce, chopped
1/4 bunch spinach, chopped
1/4 bunch cilantro, chopped
1/4 bunch green onions, chopped
1/2 cucumber, sliced
1 tomato, sliced
1/2 bunch red radishes, sliced
Marinade:
1/2 teaspoon crushed garlic
1/2 teaspoon salt
1/4 teaspoon paprika
2 tablespoons olive oil
2 tablespoons plain yogurt
1/4 teaspoon curry
1/4 teaspoon black pepper
Dressing:
3 tablespoons olive oil
2 fresh squeezed lemons
1/2 teaspoon salt

Chicken Salad, continued

1. Approximately 2 hours ahead of time mix together ingredients for marinade. Wash chicken, removing skin and fat. Place chicken in marinade, cover and let sit in refrigerator for 2 hours.

2. Wash all vegetables. Chop the lettuce, spinach, cilantro and green onions. Slice the tomato, cucumber and radishes. Place in a large bowl. Refrigerate.

3. Mix together ingredients for dressing and set aside.

4. Heat coals to medium hot.

5. Barbecue chicken over coals for 10 minutes on each side. Combine dressing with salad and toss. Cut chicken into small pieces and place on top of salad.

To Serve: with naan or pita bread.

Pepper & Tomato Salad

2 medium green bell peppers
4 medium tomatoes
1/2 bunch green onions
Dressing:
1/3 cup olive oil
2 tablespoons apple cider vinegar
salt and pepper (to taste)

1. Wash and slice peppers and tomatoes (remove seeds). Wash and chop green onions.

2. Place peppers, tomatoes and green onions in serving bowl.

3. Mix together ingredients for dressing. Toss the salad and season to taste.

Afghani Salat

1/2 bunch cilantro
1/2 head Romaine lettuce
1/2 head lettuce
1/2 bunch green onions
2 medium tomatoes
1 cucumber
5 red radishes
1 jalepeno pepper (optional)
Dressing:
1 1/2 lemons, squeezed
3 tablespoons olive oil
salt (to taste)

1. Wash all vegetables.

2. Chop all greens, onions, tomatoes, radishes and jalepeno pepper, and put into a large bowl.

3. Peel cucumber and cut into 4 pieces. With a knife peel a 1/4-inch layer around each cucumber piece until you reach seeded area in center and stop. Dispose of center seeds. Roll cucumber back into original shape and cut 1/4-inch strips. Each strip will be approximately 3 inches in length and will be curly. Add to salad bowl.

4. Mix together ingredients for dressing, pour over salad and toss.

To Serve: with naan or pita bread.

Taboule Salad

1/4 cup cracked wheat (bulgur wheat)
2 large bunches parsley
1 bunch green onions
3 medium tomatoes
3/4 cup water
Dressing:
2 medium lemons, squeezed
2 tablespoons olive oil
1 teaspoon salt

1. Soak bulgur wheat in water while you prepare the rest of the salad.

2. Wash parsley and onions. Remove stems from parsley and discard. Chop parsley and green onions into small pieces.

3. Wash tomatoes and remove seeds. Cut into small cubed pieces.

4. Mix dressing ingredients together in a bowl: juice of 2 lemons with seeds removed, olive oil and salt.

5. Strain bulgur wheat.

6. Put all ingredients together in a large bowl, pour dressing over salad and toss.

To Serve: with naan or pita bread

Da Afghan House Salad Dressing

1 cup mayonnaise
1/4 cup mustard
1/3 cup plain yogurt
1 tablespoon apple cider vinegar
1 tablespoon water
1/2 teaspoon salt
1 teaspoon dry mint leaves, crushed

1. Mix all ingredients together with a hand mixer or food processor. Refrigerate.

Soups

Rice Soup

1/2 cup long grain rice
1 small yellow onion
1 pound chicken breasts
6 cups water
1 teaspoon crushed garlic
1 teaspoon salt
2 medium carrots, chopped
1 medium potato, chopped
1/2 bunch spinach, chopped
1 teaspoon powdered dill weed
1/2 teaspoon black pepper
1 fresh lemon, squeezed

1. Wash rice and boil for 20-25 minutes until tender.

2. Peel and grind onion in a food processor or blender with 1/2 cup water.

3. Wash chicken, removing skin and fat.

4. In a soup pot put 6 cups water, chicken, onion mixture, garlic and salt. Bring to a boil and continue cooking over medium heat for 30 minutes.

5. Remove chicken, cut into small pieces and return to pot. If water reduces add more.

6. Wash and chop carrots, potato and spinach. Add to soup along with the rest of the ingredients and simmer for another 20 minutes.

To Serve: with naan or pita bread.

Bean Soup Moshawa

1 cup mung beans
1 cup garbanzo beans, drained
1 cup kidney beans, drained
1 medium onion
1/2 pound ground beef - 90% lean
1 6-oz. can tomato paste
1 teaspoon crushed garlic
2 1/2 teaspoons salt
1 tablespoon freshly ground coriander seeds
1/2 teaspoon cayenne pepper
1/2 teaspoon black pepper
6 cups water
Thickener:
2 cups plain yogurt
1/2 cup water
2 tablespoons cornstarch
2 tablespoons flour
Garnish:
dry mint

Soups

Bean Soup Moshawa, continued

1. Rinse mung beans, put in a saucepan with 3 cups of water and bring to a boil. Simmer for 20-25 minutes or until the beans are soft. Drain and set aside.

2. Brown ground beef in frying pan.

3. Peel onion, quarter and put in a food processor or blender with 1/2 cup water and grind it.

4. Add onion mixture, salt and garlic to ground beef. Saute for 10-15 minutes. Add 1 cup water and 6 oz. tomato paste. Continue to simmer for another 10 minutes.

5. Pour hamburger/tomato sauce into soup pot and add 6 cups water, garbanzo beans, kidney beans, mung beans, coriander, cayenne pepper and black pepper; bring to a boil and then simmer for 15 minutes.

6. For thickener: in a blender thoroughly mix the yogurt, water, cornstarch and flour. Add to the soup and continue cooking over low heat until hot — do not boil.

To Serve: with naan or pita bread. Garnish with dry mint.

Chicken Soup

1 whole chicken
1 medium yellow onion
2 cloves garlic, chopped
1 teaspoon salt
2 carrots
1/2 cup green beans
1 potato
6 cups water
1 fresh lemon, squeezed

1. Wash chicken and remove skin and fat. Cut chicken into small pieces and place in a soup pot with bones.

2. Peel onion and grind in a food processor or blender with 1 cup of water.

3. Boil the chicken with 6 cups water, onion mixture, salt and garlic until the chicken and onion become tender, approximately 20 minutes. With a spoon remove residue floating on top of water. (If the water reduces too much, add more.) Remove bones.

4. Peel carrots and slice into small pieces; wash green beans and cut into 1/2-inch pieces.

5. Add the carrots and green beans to the soup and let simmer while you peel and cut potato into small pieces. Add potato to soup.

Chicken Soup, continued

6. Cut lemon in half and squeeze juice into a bowl. Remove seeds and add juice to soup.

7. Cover soup and continue simmering for an additional 20-25 minutes or until vegetables are tender.

To Serve: with naan or pita bread. Garnish with black pepper

Chicken Soup with Noodles

1 pound chicken breasts
1 medium yellow onion, chopped
4 pints water
1 teaspoon crushed garlic
1 jalepeno pepper, chopped
1 1/2 teaspoons salt
1 16-oz. package frozen vegetables (your choice)
1/2 teaspoon black pepper
2 teaspoons freshly ground coriander seeds
1 5-oz. package egg noodles

1. Put in large soup pot: water, chicken (washed with skin and fat removed), onion, garlic, jalepeno pepper and salt. Cover and bring to a boil. Continue cooking over medium heat for 25-30 minutes or until onions are transparent and chicken is tender.

2. Remove chicken from pot and cut into small pieces.

3. Put chicken back into pot and add remaining ingredients— except egg noodles. Continue cooking for 5 minutes. (Note: fresh vegetables may be substituted for the frozen. You will need to simmer soup an additional 5-10 minutes.)

4. Add egg noodles and cook over medium heat until soft— about 5-10 minutes.

To Serve: with naan or pita bread. Garnish with mint or dill.

Entrees

Aushok
(Spinach Filled Pasta)

OR WONTON WRAPPERS

1 package eggroll skins, 3 1/2" x 3 1/2" (round or square)

2 bunches fresh spinach *(OR 2 PKG FROZEN SPINACH*

1 bunch green onions

1/2 bunch cilantro, optional

2 tablespoons olive oil

1 teaspoon salt

1 teaspoon black pepper

1/2 *OR LESS* teaspoon cayenne pepper

1 tablespoon freshly ground coriander seeds

Yogurt Sauce:

1 cup plain yogurt

1/2 teaspoon crushed garlic

1/4 teaspoon salt

Korma Sauce:

Vegetarian (see page 94) Make 1/2 recipe

Or

Meat Sauce:

(see page 92)

Garnish:

1 teaspoon dry mint leaves

1. Wash and chop into small pieces spinach, green onions and cilantro.

2. Mix the greens with the spices and olive oil.

3. Place eggroll skin on working surface. Place a heaping teaspoon of spinach mixture in the middle of the eggroll skin. Using your finger, wet edges of eggroll skin with water and fold in half, sealing edges. Aushok is traditionally made with round pieces, but if you use the square skins fold into triangles.

Aushok, continued

4. Put water in the bottom of a steamer and bring to a boil. (A vegetable steamer may be used.) Spray the steaming tray with Pam® cooking spray. Place Aushok on tray. Be sure Aushok do not touch each other—they will stick. Cook for 15-20 minutes with lid on.

To Serve: Spread a thin layer of the yogurt sauce on each plate. Using tongs, put Aushok on plate and drizzle yogurt sauce over each. Drizzle korma sauce (vegetarian) or meat sauce over each Aushok and garnish with dry mint leaves.

Norenj Palow
(Chicken with Rice and Orange)

3 pounds chicken pieces
2 cups basmati rice
1/8 cup corn oil
2 1/2 teaspoons salt
3 1/2 cups water
1 tablespoon corn oil
Syrup:
1 large orange
1/2 cup water
1/4 cup white sugar
1/4 cup blanched and flaked almonds
1/4 cup blanched and flaked pistachios
1/2 teaspoon saffron (dilute in 2 tablespoons hot water)
3 tablespoons rose water
1 teaspoon ground cardamom

Norenj Palow, continued

1. Rinse the rice several times in cold water until water remains clear. Add fresh water and let soak for 30 minutes.

2. Wash chicken, removing skin and fat. Heat 1/8 cup corn oil in large frying pan over medium high heat and brown chicken. Drain excess oil. Put chicken, 2 1/2 teaspoons salt and 3 1/2 cups water into a large cooking pot. Bring to a boil, cover and cook over medium heat for approximately 30 minutes or until chicken is tender.

3. While meat is cooking grate the rind of one large orange. Set aside.

4. To make the syrup: bring 1/2 cup water and 1/4 cup sugar to a boil. Add orange rind, almonds and pistachios. Boil for 5 minutes. Strain and set aside orange rind and nuts. Add saffron and rose water to the syrup and simmer for 5 minutes. Add cardamom. Set aside.

5. Remove chicken from broth and set in a warm place. Add syrup to broth and bring to a boil. Add strained rice, 1 tablespoon corn oil and half of the orange rinds and nuts, reserving the rest for garnish. Bring to a boil and then simmer until rice has absorbed all the liquid.

To Serve: Take about a quarter of the rice and put on a large serving dish. Top with the meat and then cover with the remaining rice. Garnish the top with the rest of the nuts and orange rind.

Lamb & Mushrooms

2 pounds lamb with bone
1 medium yellow onion
1/4 cup corn oil
2 1/2 cups water
1 teaspoon crushed garlic
1 teaspoon salt
3 pints fresh mushrooms
2 fresh tomatoes
1 6-oz. can tomato paste
1 green bell pepper, sliced
1 jalapeno pepper, chopped
1/2 teaspoon black pepper
Garnish:
3 stems fresh rhubarb

1. Peel and slice onion. Heat corn oil in a large frying pan over medium-high heat and saute onion until lightly browned. Drain oil and set onions aside.

2. Heat 1 tablespoon corn oil in frying pan. Add lamb and brown.

3. Transfer lamb to a large cooking pot and add water, garlic and salt. Simmer for 30-45 minutes.

4. Wash mushrooms and tomatoes and slice into thin pieces. Add mushrooms and fresh tomatoes to lamb and cook for another 15 minutes.

5. Add tomato paste, sliced green pepper, chopped jalapeno pepper and black pepper to lamb mixture and continue cooking for 15 minutes.

Lamb & Mushrooms, continued

6. Rhubarb—this will be used as a garnish on top of the dish. Cut the rhubarb into 3-inch pieces and simmer in a pot of boiling water until tender—approximately 1-2 minutes.

To Serve: with chalow (basmati rice).

Lamb & Spinach

2 pounds lamb pieces
1 medium yellow onion, sliced
1/4 cup corn oil
1 teaspoon salt
1 teaspoon crushed garlic
2 teaspoons freshly ground coriander seeds
1/2 cup water
3 bunches spinach
1 bunch green onions
1 bunch cilantro (optional)
1 jalapeno pepper (optional)
Garnish:
1 stem fresh rhubarb

1. Heat corn oil in a large frying pan and saute sliced yellow onion until lightly browned. Drain oil and set onions aside.

2. Put lamb in frying pan and brown. Add garlic, salt, coriander, fried onions and 1/2 cup water to meat and simmer for 20 minutes or until liquid is diminished.

3. While the meat is cooking, wash and finely chop the

Lamb & Spinach, continued

spinach, green onions, cilantro and hot pepper. Add this mixture to the pan with the lamb and continue cooking for 5 minutes.

4. Rhubarb—this will be used as a garnish on top of the dish. Cut the rhubarb into 2-inch pieces and simmer in a pot of boiling water until tender—approximately 1-2 minutes.

To Serve: with chalow (basmati rice).

Lamb Shank

4 lamb shanks
2 medium yellow onions
3 pints water
1 tablespoon crushed garlic
1 tablespoon salt
1 teaspoon curry powder
1/2 red bell pepper
1/2 green bell pepper
1 cup garbanzo beans
4 pita bread
Onion Marinade:
1 red onion, sliced
1/2 cup apple cider vinegar
1/2 teaspoon salt
1/2 teaspoon dry mint leaves
1/2 teaspoon black pepper

Lamb Shank, continued

1. Wash lamb shank and boil in water for 5 minutes. Discard water.

2. Slice 2 yellow onions very thin.

3. Put lamb shank in a large pot with 3 pints of clean water, sliced yellow onions, garlic, salt and curry. Boil 30-40 minutes or until the meat becomes tender. Add more water if it decreases.

4. Slice the red and green peppers, and add to pot with meat. Boil for an additional 5 minutes.

5. While the lamb is boiling, mix together ingredients for onion marinade in a small bowl.

6. Heat garbanzo beans in a saucepan with a little water. Drain.

To Serve: Put each pita bread open faced on a plate. Put a lamb shank on each pita and pour some of the meat juice over each. On one side of the plate put a portion of marinated red onions and on the other side of the plate some garbanzo beans.

Stuffed Cabbage

1 large head cabbage
1 pound lean ground beef
1 medium yellow onion, chopped
1 jalapeno pepper, chopped
1 teaspoon crushed garlic
1 cup water
1 teaspoon salt
1/4 teaspoon black pepper
2 tablespoons tomato paste
Tomato Sauce:
1 1/2 cups tomato juice
1 tomato, thinly sliced
3 tablespoons sugar
3 tablespoons fresh lime juice

Preheat oven to 350 degrees.

1. Peel and chop onion; wash and chop jalapeno pepper—discard seeds.

2. In a large frying pan brown the ground beef, onion, jalapeno pepper and garlic. Add 1 cup water and continue to cook until water is reduced. Add salt, black pepper and tomato paste. Simmer over very low heat.

3. Fill a large pot with water and bring to boil. Remove whole leaves from cabbage, rinse and boil for 5 minutes. Drain and run cool water over leaves.

4. Spray a large shallow baking dish with Pam® cooking spray. Cover the bottom of the baking dish with two layers of cabbage leaves.

5. Put a mound of beef mixture in center of each remaining

Stuffed Cabbage, continued

leaf. Firmly roll and fold leaves over so that filling will not spill out. Arrange stuffed leaves side by side, seam side down, in baking dish.

6. Combine ingredients for tomato sauce and pour over stuffed cabbage leaves in baking dish. Bake 1 1/2 hours covered and 30 minutes uncovered.

To Serve: with rice, naan or pita bread

Bonjan Chalow
(Stewed Beef and Eggplant)

2 pounds lamb or beef
1 medium eggplant
1 medium yellow onion, chopped
1/4 cup corn oil
1 teaspoon crushed garlic
1 teaspoon salt
1/2 cup water
2 medium fresh tomatoes, sliced
1 teaspoon freshly ground coriander seeds
1 teaspoon black pepper
1 jalapeno pepper, chopped
1/2 green bell pepper, chopped
1/2 red bell pepper, chopped

1. Heat corn oil in a large frying pan. Add the chopped onions and fry over medium-high heat until lightly browned. Drain oil.

2. Cut meat into 2-inch pieces and wash. Add meat, garlic and

Bonjan Chalow, continued

salt to the onions. Cook over medium heat until meat is browned.

3. Peel and chop the eggplant into 1-inch cubes. In a different frying pan, sprayed with Pam® cooking spray, lightly brown eggplant cubes over medium heat. (We do not recommend you use oil to saute eggplant, because the eggplant acts like a sponge and will soak up all the oil in the frying pan.)

4. Add to meat mixture: 1 cup water, sliced tomatoes, chopped peppers, browned eggplant and remaining spices. Continue to cook over medium-low heat for 20-25 minutes until eggplant is tender.

To Serve: with chalow (basmati rice), naan or pita bread.

Chicken Sandwich

1 pound boneless breast of chicken
1 tomato, sliced
1/4 medium yellow onion, sliced
pocket bread
White Cucumber Sauce:
(See page 93)
Marinade:
1/2 teaspoon saffron (dissolve in 2 tablespoons
of hot water)
1 tablespoon crushed garlic
1 tablespoon corn oil
1/2 teaspoon salt
1/2 tablespoon freshly ground coriander seeds
2 tablespoons plain yogurt

1. Cut chicken into 3-inch pieces.

2. Mix together ingredients for marinade in a small bowl.

3. Combine chicken with marinade. Cover and marinate in refrigerator for 3-4 hours.

4. Barbecue chicken over medium-hot coals for 8-10 minutes.

To Serve: Stuff each piece of pocket bread with some chicken, sliced tomatoes and sliced onion. Pour white cucumber sauce over each.

Morgh Roast
(Chicken with Vegetables and Rice)

3 pounds mixed chicken pieces
1 tablespoon corn oil
3 medium potatoes
3 medium carrots
1 tomato, sliced
1 green bell pepper, sliced
Tomato Sauce:
1 3/4 cups water
1 6-oz. can tomato paste
1 tablespoon crushed garlic
1 teaspoon salt
1 teaspoon freshly ground coriander seeds
1 teaspoon black pepper
1/4 teaspoon cayenne pepper (optional)

Preheat oven to 400 degrees.

1. Wash chicken, removing skin and fat.

2. Heat oil in a large frying pan over medium heat and brown chicken.

3. Peel the potatoes and carrots and cut in quarters.

4. In a greased baking dish layer the chicken, sliced tomato, sliced green pepper, potatoes and carrots.

5. Mix together all ingredients for tomato sauce and pour over chicken in baking dish. Cover and bake at 400 degrees for 1 hour.

To Serve: with chalow (basmati rice).

Lamb Chops

8 lamb chops
1/2 medium yellow onion
1 green pepper
Marinade:
3 cloves garlic
2 tablespoons corn oil
1 medium yellow onion
1 teaspoon salt
1/2 tablespoon paprika
1 tablespoon freshly ground coriander seeds

1. Put ingredients for marinade in a food processor or blender and mix for 2-3 minutes.

2. Combine lamb chops with marinade. Refrigerate for 4 hours.

3. Heat coals.

4. Barbecue meat over medium coals for 10-15 minutes. Put cut up pieces of the other onion and the green pepper on skewers and barbecue for 5 minutes.

To Serve: with chalow (basmati rice) and naan or pita bread. The Afghani Salat is a very good complement to this dish.

Kofta Chalow
(Meatballs with Rice)

1 1/2 pounds lean ground beef or lamb or mixed
2 small yellow onions
2 teaspoons crushed garlic
2 teaspoons freshly ground coriander seeds
1 teaspoon black pepper
1 teaspoon salt
1 8-oz. can tomato sauce

1. Peel one of the onions and chop into small pieces.

2. Mix chopped onion and half of the spices (garlic, coriander, black pepper and salt) with the ground meat. Shape meat into balls about 1/2-inch in diameter.

3. Peel and quarter the other onion and grind in a food processor or blender with 1/2 cup water.

4. In a large frying pan simmer the ground onion mixture and 1 teaspoon garlic for 10 minutes.

5. Add 2 cups water to the onion mixture in frying pan and place meatballs in one at a time in a single layer. Cook for 20 minutes over medium heat.

6. Add tomato sauce and other half of the spices and cook for another 15-20 minutes over medium heat.

To Serve: with naan or pita bread and chalow (basmati rice).

Bahnjean Bouranee
(Baked Eggplant)

2 medium eggplants
2 tomatoes, sliced
1 green bell pepper, sliced
Tomato Sauce:
1/2 cup tomato paste
1/2 cup water
1 teaspoon crushed garlic
1/2 teaspoon salt
1/4 teaspoon black pepper
1/4 teaspoon cayenne pepper
1 teaspoon freshly ground coriander seeds
Yogurt Sauce:
1/2 cup plain yogurt
1/4 teaspoon crushed garlic
1/4 teaspoon salt
Garnish:
1 teaspoon dry mint leaves, crushed

Preheat oven to 400 degrees.

1. Peel eggplant and slice into 1/2-inch round pieces.

2. Spray a large frying pan with Pam® cooking spray and brown eggplant over medium heat.

3. Spray a 9 x 13-baking dish with Pam® cooking spray and layer with eggplant, sliced tomatoes and green peppers.

4. Mix together all ingredients for tomato sauce. Pour sauce on top of eggplant in baking dish, cover and bake at 400 degrees for 30 minutes.

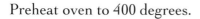

Bahnjean Bouranee, continued

5. Mix together all ingredients for yogurt sauce.

To Serve: Put a portion of the eggplant dish on a plate, pour 2 tablespoons of yogurt sauce over the top and sprinkle with dry mint leaves.

White Fish

1 pound white fish
1 1/2 cups corn oil
Marinade:
1 tablespoon crushed garlic
1/2 lemon, fresh squeezed
1 tablespoon olive oil
1 teaspoon coriander
1 teaspoon salt
1/2 teaspoon paprika
1/8 teaspoon cayenne pepper
Flour Mixture:
4 tablespoons flour
1 teaspoon freshly ground coriander seeds
1/2 teaspoon paprika
1/4 teaspoon black pepper
1/8 teaspoon cayenne pepper
Garnish:
lemon
tomatoes
parsley

White Fish, continued

1. One hour before serving mix together ingredients for marinade. Cut fish into serving size pieces. Put fish in a small bowl, cover with marinade and refrigerate for 1 hour.

2. Mix together ingredients for flour mixture.

3. Heat oil in frying pan to hot.

4. Dip fish into flour mixture and place in hot oil. Fry approximately 2 minutes on each side.

To Serve: with chalow (basmati rice) and naan or pita bread. Garnish with lemons, tomatoes and parsley.

Chicken Korma

4 pounds chicken pieces
2 medium yellow onions, sliced
1/2 cup corn oil
2 cups water
1 tablespoon crushed garlic
1 teaspoon salt
1 6-oz. can tomato paste
1 jalapeno pepper, chopped

1. Heat oil in a large frying pan over medium-high heat and saute sliced onions until lightly browned. Drain oil.

2. Remove skin and fat from chicken and wash.

3. Add the chicken, garlic, salt and water to fry pan; cover and cook for 25 minutes over medium heat.

Chicken Korma, continued

4. Take the chicken out of the onion mixture and place on a separate dish. Put the onion mixture and tomato paste in a food processor or blender and blend well.

5. Put the chicken back in the frying pan with the blended onion/tomato mixture and chopped jalapeno pepper. Continue to cook over medium-low heat for 30 minutes.

To Serve: with chalow (basmati rice).

Mantou
(Meat Filled Pasta)

1 pound ground beef or lamb—90% lean
2 medium yellow onions, chopped
1/4 green bell pepper, chopped
1 tablespoon crushed garlic
1 teaspoon salt
1 tablespoon freshly ground coriander seeds
1/2 teaspoon black pepper
1 1/4 cups water
1 package square eggroll skins, 3 1/2" x 3 1/2"
Yogurt Sauce:
1 cup plain yogurt
1/4 teaspoon salt
1/2 teaspoon crushed garlic
Tomato Sauce:
1/2 medium yellow onion
1 1/2 cups water
1 8-oz. can tomato sauce
1 1/2 teaspoons corn oil
1/2 teaspoon salt
1/2 teaspoon freshly ground coriander seeds

Mantou, continued

1/8 teaspoon black pepper
1 small carrot
1/2 cup canned garbanzo beans, strained
Garnish:
1 teaspoon dry mint leaves
1 bunch fresh cilantro

1. In a large frying pan cook over medium heat the meat, garlic, salt, coriander and black pepper until browned. Add 1 1/4 cup water and continue to cook until water is reduced.

2. Chop the onions and green bell pepper, removing seeds, and add to meat. Cook an additional 5 minutes. Remove from heat and let cool.

3. Put 1 tablespoon of meat mixture into the center of eggroll square. Wet edges of eggroll skin with water and pull 2 opposite corners together in the center and firmly seal them together. Next, seal together the 2 remaining corners to the center. Attach 2 end corners on each side to each other.

4. Put water in the bottom a steamer and bring to a boil. (A vegetable steamer may be used.) Spray the steaming tray with Pam® cooking spray. Place mantou on tray. Be sure mantou do not touch each other—they will stick. Cook for 15-20 minutes with lid on.

5. To make tomato sauce: Peel and slice the onion into very thin pieces. Boil onion in 1 1/2 cups of water for 15 minutes or until onions are tender. Strain water. Put onion, tomato sauce, corn oil, salt, coriender and black pepper into blender and blend until smooth. Put sauce back into saucepan. Peel carrot and chop into small cubes. Add carrot cubes and

Mantou, continued

strained garbanzo beans to sauce. Let simmer until carrots are tender.

To Serve: Spread a thin layer of of the yogurt sauce on each plate. Using tongs put Mantou on plate, and drizzle yogurt sauce over each Mantou. Drizzle tomato sauce over each Mantou and garnish with dry mint leaves and cilantro

Lamb Tongue

6 lamb tongues
Lamb Broth:
1 small onion, thinly sliced
2 teaspoons crushed garlic
1/2 teaspoon black pepper
2 tablespoons tomato paste
Tomato Sauce:
1/4 cup corn oil
1 teaspoon crushed garlic
1 small onion, thinly sliced
2 tomatoes, thinly sliced
1 pint mushrooms, thinly sliced
2 tablespoons tomato paste
3 tablespoons plain yogurt
1 tablespoon corn starch
1 lime, juice of
salt and pepper (to taste)

Lamb Tongue, continued

1. Rinse tongues with cold water and put in a large cooking pot with enough water to cover them along with the ingredients for the Lamb Broth. Bring to a boil, cover and simmer for 2 or 2 1/2 hours. Remove from heat. Take the tongues out of the liquid and let cool a bit. Retain liquid.

2. After the tongues have cooled, remove the outer skin. Cut each tongue into thin slices.

3. Tomato Sauce: Heat the oil in a large frying pan over medium-high heat and saute the garlic, onion, tomatoes and mushrooms. Drain any excess oil.

4. In a bowl, put 1 cup of the retained lamb broth and the rest of the ingredients for the tomato sauce: tomato paste, yogurt, corn starch, lime juice and salt and pepper. Mix well and add to vegetables in frying pan. Add tongue to frying pan and simmer for 5-10 minutes.

To Serve: Arrange tongue on a serving platter and pour sauce over it.

Fish Korma

2 pounds white fish
2 medium yellow onions
1/2 cup corn oil
1/8 cup corn oil
1 jalapeno pepper, chopped
2 cloves garlic, crushed
1 teaspoon salt
1/2 teaspoon black pepper
1 tablespoon freshly ground coriander seeds
1 8-oz. can tomato sauce
Garnish
chopped cilantro
fresh lemon

1. Thinly slice onions and fry in 1/2 cup corn oil until lightly browned. Drain oil and set onions aside.

2. Cut fish into 2-inch pieces and lightly saute in 1/8 cup corn oil in a frying pan for approximately 5 minutes. Drain oil.

3. Add onions, and the rest of the ingredients (except garnish) to fish. Cover and simmer for 15 minutes.

To Serve: with chalow (basmati rice). Garnish with freshly chopped cilantro and fresh lemon juice.

Leg of Lamb

1 boneless leg of lamb
1/3 cup corn starch
1 fresh lemon, squeezed
5 cups water
Marinade:
2 tablespoons crushed garlic
1 tablespoon salt
1 tablespoon corn oil
1/2 tablespoon paprika
1 tablespoon black pepper
1 tablespoon freshly ground coriander seeds
1/4 teaspoon cayenne pepper
1/4 cup water

1. Insert the end of a knife 8-12 times in different areas of the meat.

2. Mix together the ingredients for the marinade in a small bowl. With your hands rub the marinade onto the meat. Cover and refrigerate for 1 hour.

3. Preheat oven to 450 degrees — set to broil.

4. Place the meat into a 4-inch deep baking dish and broil on each side for 10-15 minutes, or until browned. Remove the dish from the oven.

5. Mix together lemon, water and corn starch. Pour the ingredients over the meat. Cover with foil and bake in oven at 375 degrees for 1-2 hours.

To Serve: Slice the meat and pour the juice on top of meat. Serve with rice, vegetables and baked potatoes.

Kabeli Palow
(Chicken with Raisins, Carrots and Rice)

3 pounds chicken
2 cups basmati rice
1 yellow onion, sliced
1/4 cup corn oil
2 tablespoons tomato paste
2 1/2 teaspoons salt
1 teaspoon crushed garlic
3 1/2 cups water
1 tablespoon garam masala
Garnish:
2 shredded or shaved carrots
3 tablespoons corn oil
1/2 cup raisins
1/3 cup slivered almonds
1/2 cup water

1. Rinse the rice several times in cold water until water remains clear. Add fresh water and let soak for 30 minutes.

2. Heat 1/4 cup oil in a large frying pan over medium-high heat. Cook sliced onion until dark brown. Remove onions from the oil and set aside, retain oil in pan.

3. Wash chicken removing skin and fat. Add chicken to the frying pan the onions had been in and brown well on all sides. When browned, drain excess oil. Put chicken, 2 teaspoons salt, garlic and 3 1/2 cups water into a large cooking pot. Bring to a boil, cover and cook over medium heat for approximately 30 minutes or until chicken is tender.

Kabeli Palow, continued

4. Remove the chicken and put in a warm place (retain liquid in pan). Grind the fried onion in a blender with 1/2 cup water, 2 tablespoons tomato paste and 1/2 teaspoon salt. Mix into the meat broth and boil for 10 minutes.

5. In a separate large saucepan boil 5 cups water. Drain the rice and add to the boiling water for 5 minutes. Drain the rice in a large strainer. Add rice and garam masala to meat broth and simmer until liquid is reduced.

6. While the rice is cooking, wash and peel the carrots and shred or shave. Heat 3 tablespoons oil over medium heat in a frying pan, add the carrots and cook gently until lightly browned and tender. Drain oil from pan. Add the raisins, slivered almonds and 1/2 cup water to the carrots and cook until all the water is reduced.

To Serve: Take about a quarter of the rice and put on a large dish. Top with the meat then cover with the remaining rice. Garnish the top with carrots, raisins and almonds.

Dam Pokht
(Chicken with Vegetables and Rice)

3 pounds chicken, mixed pieces
6 cups water
1 yellow onion, chopped
1 teaspoon crushed garlic
1 tablespoon salt
1 tablespoon corn oil
2 cups white basmati rice
1 fresh tomato, sliced
1 8-oz. can tomato sauce
1 tablespoon zerra (garam masala)
1/2 bunch spinach
3 carrots
2 medium potatoes

Preheat oven to 350 degrees.

1. Wash chicken and remove skin and fat. In a large cooking pot boil chicken in 6 cups water with onion, garlic and salt for 20-25 minutes over medium-high heat until chicken becomes tender and the onion pieces are soft and transparent.

2. Wash all vegetables. Chop spinach (remove stems). Peel and cut carrots in half and then quarter each half. Peel and cut potatoes into 1-inch cubes. Slice tomato. Add to meat mixture along with the remaining ingredients and continue to cook for 20 minutes over medium heat.

4. Put all ingredients in a large baking dish sprayed with Pam® cooking spray. The mixture should be very soupy—the rice will absorb much of the liquid during baking. Cover and bake at 350 degrees for 20-30 minutes or until most of the liquid, but not all, is absorbed.

Stuffed Eggplant

4 medium eggplants
1/2 pound lean ground beef or lamb
1 medium yellow onion
1/4 cup vegetable oil
1 teaspoon crushed garlic
1 teaspoon salt
1/4 teaspoon black pepper
1 cup cooked rice
2 tablespoons tomato paste
1 egg

Preheat oven to 350 degrees.

1. Wash eggplants and cut in half. Remove inside of eggplant leaving about 1/4-inch base on sides. Save the insides of the eggplant.

2. Chop onion into small pieces.

3. Heat vegetable oil in a large frying pan over medium high heat and saute onion and garlic until onions are tender. Drain oil.

4. Add ground meat, chopped insides of eggplant, salt and pepper. Cook until meat is browned. Add cooked rice and tomato paste and continue to cook for 4-5 minutes. Remove from heat.

5. Beat egg in a bowl and then add to meat/rice mixture.

6. Spray a large baking dish with Pam® cooking spray. Fill each eggplant with meat/rice mixture and place in baking dish. Cover with aluminum foil and bake for 1 hour.

To Serve: with naan or pita bread.

Chicken Tandori

3 pounds chicken, mixed pieces
1 tablespoon corn oil
1 tablespoon crushed garlic
1 teaspoon salt
1 teaspoon black pepper
1/2 teaspoon cayenne pepper
1 tablespoon chicken tandori masala*
2 teaspoons paprika
2 teaspoons freshly ground coriander seeds
1/3 cup corn starch
1 lemon, squeezed
3 cups water

Preheat oven to 375 degrees.

1. Remove skin and fat from chicken, wash and cut into small pieces.

2. In a large frying pan saute chicken in 1 tablespoon oil until browned.

3. Mix all other ingredients together in a bowl. Lay all the chicken in a baking dish sprayed with Pam® cooking spray, pour ingredients in bowl over chicken. Cover with foil, bake in oven at 375 degrees for 45 minutes.

To Serve: with chalow (basmati rice).

* Chicken tandori masala can be purchased at an Indian, Middle Eastern or Asian grocery store.

Vegetable Platter

1/2 cup cabbage
1/2 cup broccoli
1/2 cup carrots
1/2 cup green beans
1/2 cup fresh spinach
1 cup water
1 teaspoon crushed garlic
1/4 teaspoon paprika
1/4 teaspoon black pepper
1/8 teaspoon cayenne pepper
1/2 teaspoon salt
1 1/2 tablespoons olive oil
Chalow (Basmati Rice):
(See page 135)

1. Wash all vegetables and cut into serving size pieces. Put all vegetables into large fry pan with 1 cup water and bring to a boil. Simmer for 5 minutes.

2. Put remaining ingredients except rice in with vegetables and simmer until water reduces. Do not overcook.

To Serve: Spread chalow (basmati rice) on serving dish. Pour vegetables in center of rice.

Morgh Lawand
(Chicken with Rice)

3 pounds chicken, mixed pieces
1 medium yellow onion
1/4 cup corn oil
2 teaspoons crushed garlic
3 cups water
1 1/2 teaspoons salt
1/2 teaspoon cayenne pepper
1/2 teaspoon black pepper
1 tablespoon freshly ground coriander seeds
2 teaspoons curry powder
1 bunch cilantro, chopped
Sauce:
2 cups plain yogurt
1 tablespoon flour
1 6-oz. can tomato paste

1. Peel and slice onion into thin pieces. Heat oil in large frying pan over medium-high heat. Saute onions until brown. Drain oil. Remove onion from pan and blend in food processor or blender with all ingredients except chicken, cilantro and ingredients for the sauce.

2. Wash chicken, removing skin and fat. Heat 1 tablespoon oil in frying pan and brown chicken.

3. Put chicken in a larger cooking pot. Add the ingredients you mixed in food processor or blender to the chicken pieces, cover and cook over medium heat for 20 minutes.

4. To make the sauce: mix the yogurt, flour and tomato paste in a food processor or blender. (You may need to add 1/4 cup water to get mixture to blend.) Pour over chicken and continue to cook. While cooking, chop cilantro—add to chicken and continue cooking for another 15 minutes over low heat.

To Serve: serve with chalow (basmati rice).

Kabobs

Chicken Kabob

2 pounds boneless breast of chicken
1 medium yellow onion
1 green bell pepper
12 cherry tomatoes
Marinade:
1/2 teaspoon saffron (dissolve in 2 tablespoons of hot water)
1 tablespoon crushed garlic
1 tablespoon corn oil
1 teaspoon salt
1/2 tablespoon freshly ground coriander seeds
2 tablespoons plain yogurt

1. Cut chicken into 2-inch pieces.

2. Mix together ingredients for marinade in a bowl.

3. Combine chicken with marinade. Cover and marinate in refrigerator for 3-4 hours.

4. Put marinated meat on skewers. On other skewers put cut up pieces of onion, green bell pepper and cherry tomatoes.

5. Cook meat on the barbecue for 10-15 minutes over medium-hot coals. Cook the vegetables for 5 minutes.

To Serve: with naan or pita bread, Afghani salat and chutney sauces.

Kabobi Dosh(Stovetop)
(Beef with Onions)

2 pounds beef without bones
1 tablespoon corn oil
3 medium yellow onions
2 cloves crushed garlic
1 teaspoon salt
1 cup water
1/4 cup apple cider vinegar
1 teaspoon black pepper

1. Cut meat into 2-inch squares.

2. Heat corn oil in a large frying pan and brown meat.

3. Add water, garlic and salt to meat mixture, cover and cook for 20 minutes over medium heat.

4. Slice onions very thin and add to meat mixture in pan. Cook for 10 minutes.

5. Add vinegar and black pepper and cook for another 5 minutes or until water and vinegar are reduced.

To Serve: with naan or pita bread and chalow (basmati rice).

Fish Kabob

1 pound sword fish
Marinade:
1 tablespoon crushed garlic
1/2 fresh squeezed lemon
1 tablespoon olive oil
1 tablespoon freshly ground coriander seeds
1 teaspoon salt
1/4 teaspoon black pepper
1/2 teaspoon paprika
1/8 teaspoon cayenne pepper

1. Cut fish into 2-inch pieces.
2. Mix together ingredients for marinade in a small bowl. Put fish in a small bowl, cover with marinade and let sit for 1 hour.
3. Put fish on skewers and barbecue over hot coals for 5-7 minutes. (Do not overcook.)

To Serve: with baked potatoes, vegetables and yogurt and cilantro chutney.

Lamb Kabob

2 pounds lamb pieces (from leg section, no bone)
1 medium yellow onion
1 green bell pepper
12 cherry tomatoes
Marinade:
1 tablespoon crushed garlic
1 tablespoon corn oil
1 1/2 teaspoons salt
1 tablespoon freshly ground coriander seeds
2 tablespoons plain yogurt

1. Cut lamb into 2-inch pieces.
2. Mix together ingredients for marinade in a bowl.
3. Combine lamb with marinade. Cover and marinate in refrigerator for 2 hours.
4. Put marinated meat on skewers. On other skewers put cut up pieces of onion, green bell pepper and cherry tomatoes.
5. Cook meat on the barbecue for 10-15 minutes over medium-hot coals. Cook the vegetables for 5 minutes.

To Serve: with chalow (basmati rice), naan or pita bread and tomato chutney.

Beef Kabob

2 pounds beef tenderloin
Marinade:
1/2 medium yellow onion
2 tablespoons plain yogurt
1 tablespoon crushed garlic
1 tablespoon corn oil
1 tablespoon salt
1 tablespoon freshly ground coriander seeds
1/2 teaspoon black pepper

1. Cut beef into 2-inch cubes.

2. Put ingredients for marinade in a food processor or blender and mix for 2-3 minutes.

3. Combine cut meat with marinade. Cover and refrigerate for 2 hours.

4. Put meat on metal skewers and cook on the barbecue for 10-15 minutes over medium-hot coals.

To Serve: with vegetable kabob, pita bread, chalow (basmati rice), naan or pita bread and red chutney sauce.

Shrimp Kabob

1 pound shrimp (12 count)
Marinade:
1 teaspoon paprika
1 tablespoon freshly ground coriander seeds
1 tablespoon crushed garlic
1 teaspoon salt
1/2 teaspoon black pepper
1/4 teaspoon cayenne pepper
1 tablespoon corn oil
2 tablespoons plain yogurt

1. Clean and peel shrimp.
2. Put ingredients for marinade in a food processor or blender and mix for 2-3 minutes.
3. Combine shrimp with marinade. Cover and refrigerate for 2 hours.
4. Put shrimp on metal skewers and cook on the barbecue for 5-7 minutes over medium-hot coals. (Do not overcook.)

To Serve: with chalow (basmati rice), naan or pita bread, vegetables, yogurt and cilantro chutney.

Kofta Kabob

1 pound ground beef—90% lean
1 pound ground lamb
1 medium yellow onion
1/2 green bell pepper
3 cloves garlic, crushed
1 tablespoon salt
1 tablespoon freshly ground coriander seeds
1/2 teaspoon fresh ginger root, peeled
1/2 teaspoon black pepper
1/2 bunch fresh cilantro
1/4 teaspoon cayenne pepper

1. Peel onion and cut into quarters. Remove seeds from green pepper.

2. Put all ingredients except the meat into a blender and mix well.

3. Mix the blended ingredients with the ground beef and lamb.

4. Cover and refrigerate for 2 hours.

5. Take a small handful of meat and wrap around skewer. Press meat firmly to the skewers. Each kabob will be approximately 1 1/2 inches round and 4 inches long.

6. Cook on barbecue over medium hot coals for 10-15 minutes. Don't overcook.

To Serve: with tabouli salad, red chutney sauce, vegetable and pita or naan bread.

Vegetables

Beans — Yellow & Green

1/2 pound yellow beans
1/2 pound green beans
1 medium yellow onion
1/4 cup corn oil
1 teaspoon crushed garlic
1 teaspoon salt
1/4 teaspoon black pepper
1/2 cup water
1 serano pepper, chopped, seeds removed
1 fresh tomato, sliced

1. Wash beans and cut into 2-inch pieces.

2. Peel onion and cut into thin slices. Heat oil in a large frying pan over medium-high heat and saute onions until golden brown. Drain oil.

3. Add beans, garlic, salt, black pepper, water, serano pepper and fresh tomato to frying pan with onion. Cover and cook over medium-low heat for 25 minutes stirring occasionally. Water should be mostly reduced.

To Serve: with an entree, naan or pita bread and rice.

Turnips — Sweet

2 pounds turnips

1 medium yellow onion

1/4 cup corn oil

1 teaspoon crushed garlic

1/4 teaspoon salt

1 cup water

1/4 teaspoon black pepper

1 teaspoon freshly ground coriander seeds

1/2 cup sugar

1 4-oz. can tomato sauce

1. Peel the turnips, quarter and cut into thick slices. Peel onion and cut into very thin slices.

2. Heat oil in a large frying pan over medium-high heat. Saute the onion until golden brown. Drain oil.

3. Add the garlic, salt and water to the onion in the frying pan. Cook over low heat for 5-10 minutes.

4. Add the turnips and the rest of the ingredients. Cover and cook for 20 minutes until the turnips are soft and most of the liquid is reduced.

To Serve: with chalow (basmati rice) and naan or pita bread.

Pumpkins Kadu Bouranee
(Sweet Pumpkin)

1 1/2-2 pounds fresh pumpkin or squash
1/4 cup corn oil
Sweet Tomato Sauce:
1 teaspoon crushed garlic
1 cup water
1/2 teaspoon salt
1/2 cup sugar
1 4-oz. can tomato sauce
1/2 teaspoon ginger root, chopped fine
1 teaspoon freshly ground coriander seeds
1/4 teaspoon black pepper
Yogurt Sauce:
1/4 teaspoon crushed garlic
1/4 teaspoon salt
3/4 cup plain yogurt
Garnish:
dry mint leaves, crushed

1. Peel the pumpkin and cut into 2-3 inch cubed pieces, set aside.

2. Heat oil in a large frying pan that has a lid. Fry the pumpkins on both sides for a couple of minutes until lightly browned.

3. Mix together ingredients for sweet tomato sauce in a bowl and then add to pumpkin mixture in frying pan. Cover and cook for 20-25 minutes over low heat until the pumpkin is cooked and most of the liquid has evaporated.

4. Mix together the ingredients for the yogurt sauce.

To Serve: Spread half the yogurt sauce on a plate and lay the

Pumpkins Kadu Bouranee, continued

pumpkins on top. Top with remaining yogurt and any cooking juices left over. Sprinkle with dry mint. May be served with chalow (basmati rice) and naan or pita bread.

Dal — Lentil Beans

1 cup lentil beans-dry
1 3/4 cups water
1/2 teaspoon salt
1 teaspoon freshly ground coriander seeds
1/2 teaspoon curry powder
1/8 teaspoon black pepper
Dressing:
2 tablespoons olive oil
2 teaspoons crushed garlic

1. Rinse beans with cold water several times.
2. Put all ingredients into a medium size saucepan except dressing. Boil over medium heat for approximately 15 minutes or until beans are tender and most of the water is reduced.
3. To make the dressing: In a small frying pan heat the olive oil and saute the crushed garlic.
4. Pour the garlic dressing over the beans and stir well.

Subzi (Spinach)

2 bunches spinach
1 bunch cilantro (optional)
1 bunch green onions
1 hot pepper
1/4 cup corn oil
1 medium yellow onion
1 teaspoon crushed garlic
1/2 teaspoon salt
1/2 cup water
1/2 teaspoon freshly ground coriander seeds
1/2 teaspoon black pepper

1. Chop and wash the spinach, cilantro, green onions and hot pepper. Remove seeds from hot pepper.

2. Peel and slice yellow onion. Heat oil in a large frying pan over medium-high heat. Saute onions until lightly browned. Drain oil.

3. Add the garlic, salt and water and cook over medium-low heat until the water reduces and the onions become soft.

4. Add all the greens and the rest of the ingredients and cook for another 15 minutes over low heat.

To Serve: with chalow (basmati rice), plain yogurt and naan or pita bread.

Beans 'N Cream

1/2 pound dried butter beans
1 carrot, shredded
1/2 small yellow onion, chopped
1 teaspoon salt
1 teaspoon crushed garlic
1/4 cup half and half cream
pepper

1. Rinse beans several times with cold water.

2. Put beans in a large saucepan with 5 cups of water and bring to a boil. Simmer for 5 minutes. Pour beans through a strainer and rinse with cold water. Put beans back in pan and cover with cold water.

3. Add shredded carrot, chopped onion, salt and crushed garlic. Bring to a boil, cover and simmer for about 1 hour or until beans are tender. Water should reduce to a thick soupy consistency.

4. Stir in half and half.

To Serve: Garnish with pepper.

Sweet Carrots & Raisins

6 carrots
1/3 cup water
1/2 cup raisins
1 tablespoon brown sugar
1 tablespoon corn oil

1. Wash and peel carrots. Cut carrots into thin round slices.

2. Put water and carrots in a medium sized frying pan. Cover and simmer for 15 minutes. Add raisins, brown sugar and oil. Cook for approximately 5 minutes or until raisins are puffed up and carrots are tender. Water should be mostly reduced.

Karum Curry (Cabbage)

4 cups green cabbage, shredded
2 carrots, shredded
1/8 cup vegetable oil
1 small onion, chopped
1 teaspoon salt
2 teaspoons curry powder
1 teaspoon crushed garlic
1/4 cup water

1. Wash and shred cabbage and carrots.

2. Chop onion into small pieces.

3. In a large frying pan add vegetable oil, salt curry and garlic and mix well. Turn heat to low and add cabbage, carrots and onion. Stir well.

4. Add water, cover and simmer until water is reduced — approximately 5-7 minutes.

Cauliflower Bouranee

1 large head of cauliflower
1 medium yellow onion
1/4 cup corn oil
2 cups water
1 teaspoon crushed garlic
1/2 teaspoon salt
1 8-oz. can tomato sauce
1/4 teaspoon curry powder
1/2 teaspoon black pepper
1/2 teaspoon freshly ground coriander seeds
1/2 teaspoon ginger root, peeled and crushed

1. Cut the cauliflower into florets and thinly slice the onion.

2. In a large frying pan heat oil over medium-high heat. Saute onion until golden brown. Drain oil. Add the garlic, salt and 1 cup water and cook for 10-15 minutes over medium-low heat.

3. Mix together remaining ingredients in a bowl.

4. Add the cauliflower and the remaining ingredients to the frying pan and cook over medium-low heat for 15-20 minutes or until cauliflower is tender.

To Serve: with chalow (basmati rice).

Yellow Beans with Dill

2-3 cups yellow beans
1/2 small yellow onion
1/4 cup vegetable oil
1/2 cup water
1/2 teaspoon salt
1/8 teaspoon black pepper
1/2 teaspoon dillweed

1. Wash beans and cut into 2-inch pieces.

2. Peel onion and cut into thin slices. Heat oil in a large frying pan over medium-high heat and saute onions until golden brown. Drain oil.

3. Add beans, salt, black pepper, water and dill weed to frying pan with onion. Cover and cook over medium-low heat for approximately 25 minutes stirring occasionally. Water should be mostly reduced.

Vegetable Kabob

2 cups whole mushrooms
2 medium zucchini
1 medium yellow onion
1 cup cherry tomatoes
Marinade:
1/4 cup vegetable oil
1 teaspoon lemon juice
1 teaspoon crushed garlic
1/4 teaspoon black pepper

1. Wash all vegetables.

2. Cut zucchini into 3/4-inch slices (discard ends). Cut onion in quarters.

3. Put vegetables on skewers.

4. Combine all ingredients for marinade. Brush marinade over vegetables.

5. Cook vegetables over hot coals for approximately 10 minutes. Brush vegetables with marinade frequently.

To Serve: with meat kabob and naan or pita bread.

Sauces

Cilantro Chutney

1 bunch cilantro
1 clove garlic
1/2 cup apple cider vinegar
2 jalapeno peppers
2 walnuts
1 teaspoon salt

1. Wash cilantro, peel garlic and remove seeds from peppers.
2. Put all ingredients into a blender and thoroughly blend. Keep refrigerated.

To Serve: with naan bread or kebobs.

Meat Sauce

1 pound lean ground beef
1 small yellow onion
1/2 cup water
1 teaspoon crushed garlic
1 teaspoon salt
1 tablespoon freshly ground coriander seeds
1/2 teaspoon black pepper
1 16-oz. can tomato sauce
1 cup water

1. Grind onion and 1/2 cup water in a food processor or blender.

2. Mix blended onion and ground beef together and brown in frying pan over medium-high heat.

3. Add 1 cup water and remaining ingredients to meat and cook for 20-25 minutes over medium-low heat.

White Cucumber Sauce

1 cup plain yogurt
1/4 cup chopped cucumber
1/4 teaspoon salt
1/4 teaspoon crushed dry mint

1. Peel cucumber removing seeds. Chop cucumber.

2. Mix together all ingredients.

To Serve: with sambosa, boulanee, bread and sandwiches.

Korma Sauce

1 medium yellow onion
3 cups water
1 16-oz. can tomato sauce
1 tablespoon corn oil
1 teaspoon salt
1 1/2 teaspoon freshly ground coriander seeds
1/4 teaspoon black pepper

1. Slice the onion very thin. Boil the onion in 3 cups of water until the onion becomes tender, approximately 15 minutes.

2. Strain water. Put onion into a blender with remaining ingredients. Blend well.

3. Put sauce back into saucepan; bring to a boil and then simmer until sauce thickens up.

Yogurt-Cilantro Chutney

1/2 bunch cilantro
1 medium jalapeno pepper, seeds removed
2 cups of plain yogurt
1 teaspoon crushed garlic
1 teaspoon salt
1/4 cup walnuts

1. Put all ingredients in blender and blend well. Keep refrigerated.

Yogurt Sauce

1/2 cup plain yogurt
1/4 teaspoon crushed garlic
1/4 teaspoon salt
1/2 teaspoon dry mint leaves, crushed

1. Mix all ingredients together.

Tomato Chutney

1/2 red bell pepper
3 medium jalapeno peppers
1/8 cup apple cider vinegar
1 teaspoon dry mint leaves
1/2 teaspoon salt
1/2 teaspoon black pepper
1/2 teaspoon freshly ground coriander seeds
1/2 teaspoon crushed garlic
1 8-oz can tomato sauce

1. Wash red bell pepper and jalapeno peppers. Remove and discard seeds. Put peppers and vinegar in blender and blend until smooth.

2. Pour blended mixture into small saucepan with the rest of the ingredients. Bring to a boil and remove from heat. Cool and serve.

To Serve: with naan bread, appetizers, meats and kabobs

Kabob Sauce

2 cups chicken or beef broth
1/3 cup flour
2 tablespoons corn starch
1/4 cup corn oil
1 teaspoon salt
1 teaspoon black pepper
1 tablespoon paprika
1 tablespoon freshly ground coriander seeds

1. In a small saucepan heat 1/4 cup corn oil and add flour and saute until flour becomes brown. Add remaining ingredients and bring to a boil.

To Serve: with Kabobs and meats.

Desserts

New Year's Dessert

1 cup green raisins
1 cup dark seedless raisins
1 cup dry apricots
1 tablespoon rose water
3 pints water
1 cup sugar (to taste)
Nuts:
(unsalted and skinless)
1 cup walnuts
1 cup almonds
1 cup pistachios

1. Put all ingredients in a large bowl. Cover and refrigerate for 24 hours. Raisins should be swollen.

To Serve: Put a portion of fruit and nuts into small serving bowls along with some of the juice. Use a soup spoon to eat.

Ferne
(Custard)

2 cups whole milk
1/2 cup sugar
4 tablespoons cornstarch
1 teaspoon freshly ground cardamom
Garnish:
1 tablespoon pistachio nuts
sliced fresh fruit (strawberries, cherries, bananas)

1. Mix milk, sugar and cornstarch in a saucepan and bring to a boil, stirring constantly.

2. When the mixture has come to a boil, remove from stove.

3. Add cardamom.

4. Pour into a shallow serving dish and refrigerate.

To Serve: Decorate with strawberries, cherries, bananas and pistachio nuts.

Shir Brinj
(Rice Pudding)

1 cup long grain rice (do not use basmati rice)
2 cups water
2 cups whole milk
1/2 cup half and half
1 cup sugar
1 teaspoon cardamom
Garnish:
ground pistachio nuts

1. Wash rice. Put water and rice in a medium sized saucepan and bring to a boil, reduce heat and continue to cook over medium heat until rice has absorbed all water.

2. Add the remaining ingredients, bring mixture to a boil, and then simmer over medium-low heat for approximately 25 minutes stirring frequently. Remove from heat when mixture is thick and soupy.

3. Cool before serving (will thicken some during refrigeration).

To Serve: Serve in fancy serving dishes, sprinkle with pistachio nuts.

Khatae
(Cookies)

1 1/2 cups white flour
1 cup sugar
3/4 cup corn oil
1 teaspoon crushed cardamom
2 tablespoons ground pistachio nuts

Preheat oven to 350 degrees.

1. Mix the flour, sugar and cardamom.

2. Add the oil and mix well.

3. Form dough into 2-inch round balls, place on cookie sheets and then press the tip of your finger into the middle of each cookie (to resemble belly button).

4. Bake cookies for 15-20 minutes until lightly brown.

5. Sprinkle finely ground pistachio nuts on top of cookies when still hot from oven.

Heela
(Ice Cream Filled Puff Pastries)

1/2 box puff pastry sheets
1 pint vanilla ice cream
1 10-oz. package frozen strawberry pieces
1 tablespoon sugar
1/2 cup half and half
4 teaspoons ground pistachio nuts

Preheat oven to 375 degrees.

1. Using a 1-inch round cookie cutter cut out several pastry puffs (6 puffs per person). Bake at 375 degrees until lightly browned.

2. Split each puff in half so you have a top and a bottom.

3. Prepare strawberry sauce by boiling strawberries and sugar until it becomes the consistency of syrup. Set aside.

To Serve: Fill center of each pastry with 1 teaspoon of ice cream. Put 6 ice cream pastries in each serving dish. Top with 2 tablespoons of half and half, 2 tablespoons strawberry sauce and sprinkle with 1 teaspoon ground pistachio nuts.

duplicate test

Jellibe
(Sweet Pastry)

1 cup white flour
1 cup water
2 teaspoons plain yogurt
1/2 teaspoon baking soda
1 teaspoon dry yeast
2 cups oil for frying
Syrup:
1 cup water
2 cups sugar
1 tablespoon lemon juice
2 teaspoons honey
1/2 tablespoon rose water

1. Mix together flour, water, yogurt, baking soda, and yeast in a bowl and let set for 25-30 minutes at room temperature.
2. Heat oil to hot in a large frying pan to approximately 375 degrees.
3. Put batter in a container similar to a plastic mustard or ketchup bottle.
4. Hold the bottle over the oil and squeeze the batter directly into the oil into pretzel shapes. Fry on both sides until golden brown. Remove from oil and set on paper towels.
5. Put ingredients for syrup together in saucepan and bring to a boil.
6. Dip cookies into syrup and set on a rack to dry.

Magute
(Pudding)

2 cups water
1/2 cup sugar
4 tablespoons corn starch
1/4 teaspoon saffron (dissolve in 2 tablespoons of hot water)
1/2 cup slivered almonds
1/2 cup split pistachios
1 teaspoon freshly ground cardamom

1. Mix sugar, diluted saffron, water and cornstarch in a saucepan. Bring to a boil over high heat, stirring constantly with a wooden spoon.

2. Remove from stove and add nuts and cardamom.

3. Pour onto a large serving platter and let cool in refrigerator.

To Serve: surround plate with fresh fruit.

Silk Kabob

6 eggs
1-1 1/4 cups corn oil
Syrup:
3/4 cup water
3/4 cup sugar
1/2 teaspoon ground cardamom
Garnish:
2 tablespoons ground pistachio nuts

1. Beat eggs well in a bowl.

2. Mix water and sugar together in a saucepan and bring to a boil. Continue to boil until it becomes syrupy—approximately 5 minutes. Add cardamom and keep warm.

3. Heat oil in a large frying pan to hot. Dip fingers deep into bowl of eggs and let egg mixture drip into hot oil. Make "silken" strands across the length of the frying pan. Work rapidly, dipping your fingers in the egg mixture 4-5 times. With a metal spatula gently roll the egg strands into a roll. Remove from frying pan.

To Serve: Pour some of the syrup over each silk kabob and garnish by sprinkling ground pistachio nuts on top.

Baklava

1 box fillo dough (thawed)
1/2 pound unsalted butter
1 teaspoon cinnamon
1 teaspoon freshly ground cardamom
1 pound walnuts or almonds, chopped
Syrup:
1 1/2 cups water
1 1/2 cups sugar
1 teaspoon fresh lemon juice
Garnish
1/4 cup pistachios, chopped

Preheat oven to 375 degrees.

1. Melt butter in a saucepan over very low heat. Combine cinnamon and crushed cardamom in a small bowl.

2. On a baking sheet lay 2 layers of fillo dough. Pour about 2 tablespoons of melted butter over dough and using a pastry brush spread the butter all over the dough surface.

3. Lay 2 more layers of fillo over the ones you just buttered. Put another 2 tablespoons of butter on and spread with pastry brush. Spread a thin layer of crushed nuts and sprinkle with a small amount of the cinnamon and cardamom mixture.

4. Repeat steps 2 and 3 until you have several layers.

5. On the top layer spread with melted butter only. Bake in oven at 375 degrees until fillo dough is golden brown. Remove from oven and prepare syrup.

6. To make syrup: combine all ingredients for syrup and bring to a boil. Simmer for 5 minutes. When baklava is still warm,

Baklava, continued

cut into small triangle shapes and drizzle syrup over, covering all pieces of baklava. Sprinkle with crushed pistachio nuts.

Beverages

Berry Yogurt Shake

1/4 cup of your favorite berries
1/2 cup plain yogurt
1/2 cup 2% milk
1 tablespoon honey
1/4 teaspoon rose water

1. Wash berries.

2. Put all ingredients into blender and blend until smooth.

To Serve: Pour into serving glass. (1 serving)

Yogurt Drink

1 cup plain yogurt
3 cups cold water
4 tablespoons chopped cucumber
Garnish:
dry mint, crushed
salt (to taste)

1. Peel and chop cucumber into small pieces.

2. Put yogurt and water into a blender and blend until smooth.

3. Pour into serving glasses.

4. Put one tablespoon of chopped cucumber into each glass with a small amount of salt and stir.

To Serve: garnish each glass with a pinch of crushed dry mint. (4 servings)

Carrot Juice

3 medium carrots
1 apple
1 stalk celery

1. Peel carrots and wash apple and celery.
2. Cut apple into quarters, discarding seeds. Cut carrots and celery in half lengthwise.
3. Put fruit and vegetables through electronic juicer.
4. If you prefer, pour juice through strainer for a smoother drink.

To Serve: Pour into glass and enjoy. (1 serving)

Pineapple-Banana Shake

1 cup fresh pineapple
1 banana
2 teaspoons honey
2 teaspoons fresh lime juice
4-5 ice cubes partially crushed

1. Cut pineapple into 1-inch chunks and set aside.

2. Cut lime in half and squeeze juice from one half of lime into a small dish.

3. Partially crush ice cubes in blender.

4. Put all ingredients in blender and blend until smooth.

To Serve: Pour into serving glass and serve immediately. (1 serving)

Pineapple-Cucumber Juice

1 cucumber (approx. 1 cup)
1 cup fresh pineapple
3-4 ice cubes partially crushed

1. Peel cucumber and remove center seeded area.

2. Cut pineapple into 1-inch chunks.

3. Partially crush ice in blender and then add remaining ingredients—blend until smooth.

To Serve: Pour into serving glass and serve immediately. (1
serving)

Pomegranate Drink

2 ripe pomegranates (skin should be thin)

1. Split pomegranates into 4 sections. Hold the seed side facing down into a bowl and firmly tap on the outer skin. Seeds will fall out into bowl.
2. Put seeds through electronic juicer.

To Serve: Pour in glass and enjoy. (1 serving)

Apple-Pineapple Juice

1 cup fresh pineapple
1 orange
2 apples
1 teaspoon fresh lemon juice

1. Cut pineapple into chunk sized pieces that will fit into your electronic juicer, peel orange and wash apples.

2. Cut apples into quarters, discarding seeds.

3. Put pineapple, orange and apples through electronic juicer.

4. If you prefer, pour juice through strainer for a smoother drink.

5. Stir in lemon juice.

To Serve: Pour in glass and enjoy. (1 Serving)

Lesee
(Sweet Yogurt Drink)

1/2 cup plain yogurt
1/2 cup 2% milk
sugar (to taste)
2 drops rose water

1. Blend all ingredients together.

To Serve: Pour into drinking glass. (1 serving)

Kayla Shake (Banana)

1/2 banana
1/2 cup plain yogurt
1/2 cup milk
1 1/2 tablespoons honey

1. Put all ingredients into blender and blend until smooth.

To Serve: Pour into serving glass. (1 serving)

Shir Chiy
(Sweet Milk Tea)

3 cups water
3 tablespoons ground Brooke Bond Indian Calcutta Red
Label Tea
2 tablespoons sugar (to taste)
2 cups milk
Garnish:
ground cardamom

Afghans drink Shir Chiy for breakfast or with a snack in the early afternoon. Since this drink has a lot of caffeine it is seldom served in the evening.

1. Bring 3 cups water to a boil.
2. Add tea and sugar and boil for 5 minutes.
3. Add milk and bring to a boil.
4. Strain tea and pour into cups.

To Serve: Garnish each cup with a pinch of cardamom.

Green Carrot Juice

1/4 bunch parsley
4 carrots
1 apple

1. Wash parsley.

2. Wash and peel carrots.

3. Cut apples into quarters, discarding seeds.

4. Put parsley, carrots and apple through electronic juicer.

5. If you prefer, pour juice through strainer for a smoother drink.

To Serve: Pour in glass and enjoy. (1 Serving)

Orange Yogurt Drink

2 oranges
1 cup plain yogurt
2 tablespoons honey

1. Extract juice from oranges.
2. Put juice of oranges, yogurt and honey in blender and blend until smooth.

To Serve: Pour into glasses and serve immediately. (1 serving)

Apple Refresher

4 medium apples
1/2-inch piece ginger root

1. Wash apples and cut into quarters, discarding seeds.

2. Peel ginger root.

3. Put apples and ginger through electronic juicer.

4. If you prefer, pour juice through strainer for a smoother drink.

To Serve: Pour into a glass and enjoy. (1 serving)

Grape Yogurt Drink

1/2 cup grape juice
3/4 cup plain yogurt
3 ice cubes partially crushed
1 teaspoon honey

1. Partially crush ice in blender and then add remaining ingredients and blend until smooth.

To Serve: Pour into serving glass and serve immediately.
(1 serving)

Watermelon Drink

4 cups watermelon (cubed with seeds removed)
5 strawberries

1. Cut watermelon into 1-2-inch cubes, discarding seeds.

2. Wash strawberries and cut in half.

3. Put through electronic juicer.

4. If you prefer, pour juice through strainer for a smoother drink.

To Serve: Pour into a glass and enjoy. (1 serving)

Miscellaneous

Naan
(Afghani Flat Bread)

1/2 cup warm water
1/4 oz. active dry yeast
1 teaspoon sugar
3/4 cup warm water
1 cup whole wheat flour
2 cups white flour (approx.)
1 teaspoon salt
2 tablespoons sesame seeds

Preheat oven to 500 degrees.

1. In a large warm bowl, dissolve 1/4 oz. active dry yeast and 1 teaspoon sugar into 1/2 cup warm water (115-120 degrees F.) Water should feel very warm to the touch.

2. Stir in 3/4 cup of warm water.

3. Stir in flour one cup at a time. Add salt. (Mix with a spoon until mixture becomes too thick to stir. Use your hand to continue mixing in the rest of the flour.) Add just enough flour so that dough is manageable.

4. Remove dough from bowl and kneed on a floured surface until dough is smooth. You may need to add small amounts of flour as you kneed so it does not stick to your hands or surface. Kneed approximately 50 times.

5. Put in a greased bowl, cover with a cloth or plastic wrap and put in a warm place to raise. Let raise for 1 hour.

6. Spray 2 large cookie sheets with Pam® spray. Spread 1/2 dough on each cookie sheet in the shape of a large oval. Dough should be spread about 1/3 inch thick. Run your hand under cold water, spread your fingers apart and drag

your fingers through the dough making deep grooves. Sprinkle sesame seeds over dough.

7. Bake dough for about 10-12 minutes. Top of bread should be a medium golden brown. Eat bread when still warm. To store, freeze in plastic bags. To reheat, wrap bread in tinfoil and warm in oven.

To Serve: with cilantro or tomato chutney. This bread is excellent with many Afghan dishes.

Homemade Yogurt

4 cups 2% milk
2 tablespoons plain yogurt

1. Put milk in a medium sized saucepan and bring to a boil. Remove from heat.

2. Mix in plain yogurt when you can put your finger into the milk without burning yourself (approximately 110 degrees). Do not add more yogurt than what is called for.

3. Pour mixture into a bowl or serving dishes and cover with plastic wrap. Put in a warm place where there is no draft for 7-8 hours. An oven with pilot light is a good place.

4. Place in refrigerator and chill before serving. Don't forget to save some of your yogurt for your next batch. You can keep using the same culture over and over again.

Sweet Homemade Yogurt

4 cups 2% milk
2 tablespoon plain yogurt
3 tablespoons white sugar

1. Put milk in a medium sized saucepan and bring to a boil. Remove from heat.

2. Mix in plain yogurt and sugar when you can put your finger into the milk without burning yourself (approximately 110 degrees). Do not add more yogurt than what is called for.

3. Pour mixture into a bowl or serving dishes and cover. Put in a warm place where there is no draft for 7-8 hours. An oven with pilot light is a good place.

4. Place in refrigerator and chill before serving.

Variations:

Mix your favorite fruits in the yogurt. Before setting, put some fruit in the bottom of a serving dish. Pour warm yogurt over fruit, cover and put in a warm area for 7-8 hours. Chill and serve. The author prefers mixing his favorite fruits with the yogurt immediately before serving. Try different combinations.

Chalow (Basmati Rice)

2 cups basmati rice
1 cup water
1 tablespoon corn oil
1 teaspoon salt

1. Wash the rice 3 times in cold water, then soak in 3 cups of water for 20-30 minutes.

2. Boil 6 cups of water in a large saucepan. Strain the rice and put in boiling water. Boil rice for 5-6 minutes. Strain rice.

3. Put rice back in saucepan and add 1 cup water, 1 tablespoon corn oil and 1 teaspoon salt. Simmer for approximately 10 minutes or until rice has absorbed all liquid.

Index

Index